In the mud

Speed Sounds

Consonants   *Ask children to say the sounds.*

f	l ll	m	n	r	s	v	z	sh	(th)	ng nk

b	c k (ck)	d	g	h	j	p	qu	t	w	x	y	ch

Vowels   *Ask children to say the sounds in and out of order.*

a	e	i	o	u

*Each box contains one sound but sometimes more than one grapheme.
Focus graphemes for this story are **circled**.*

Ditty 1   In the mud

Story Green Words

Ask children to read the words first in Fred Talk and then say the word.

thick	black	mud
plant	sock	lots

Ask children to read the root first and then the whole word with the suffix.

dig → digs   bulb → bulbs

Red Words

Ask children to practise reading the words.

I   the   of   my   he

In the mud ☆

Introduction
A man is digging in his garden. Let's see what happens!

I dig in the thick black mud

I plant lots of bulbs

my dog digs in the thick

black mud

he digs up a sock

Ditty 2 My tip-up truck

Story Green Words

Ask children to read the words first in Fred Talk and then say the word.

tip-up	truck	full	sand
tip	help		

Red Words

Ask children to practise reading the words.

I	my	the	of

My tip-up truck

Introduction

Do you like trucks? In this story one man is driving a truck and another man gets a shock!

I am in my tip-up truck

the truck is full of sand

tip it up

help

Ditty 3   £5 to spend

Story Green Words

Ask children to read the words first in Fred Talk and then say the word.

will   truck   gran

plant   pot

Ask children to say the syllables and then read the whole word.

co|mic

Red Words

Ask children to practise reading the words.

I   my

£5 to spend

The boy in this story is deciding how to spend his £5.
What do you think he might buy?

I will not get a comic

I will not get a truck

I will get my gran

a plant in a pot

Questions to talk about

Read out each question and ask children to TTYP (turn to your partner) and discuss.

Ditty 1

What does the man plant in the mud?

What does the dog find in the mud?

Have you ever planted anything?

Ditty 2

What type of truck is it?

What is the truck full of?

Have you ever accidentally upset someone?

Ditty 3

What two things does the boy want to buy?

Why does the boy buy a plant in a pot for his gran instead?

How would you spend your £5?

Speedy Green Words

Ask children to practise reading the words across the rows, down the columns and in and out of order clearly and quickly.

in	up	am	a
is	it	not	get